# Ape's *Adventure*

## in Alphabet Town

by *Janet McDonnell*
*illustrated by Linda Hohag*

created by Wing Park Publishers

CHILDRENS PRESS ®

CHICAGO

**Library of Congress Cataloging-in-Publication Data**

McDonnell, Janet, 1962-
 Ape's adventure in Alphabet Town / by Janet McDonnell ;
illustrated by Linda Hohag.
     p.    cm. — (Read around Alphabet Town)
 Summary: Ape meets "a" words on her adventure in
Alphabet Town. Includes activities.
  ISBN 0-516-05401-5
 [1. Alphabet—Fiction.   2. Apes—Fiction.]   I. Hohag, Linda, ill.
II. Title.   III. Series.
PZ7.M478436An   1992
[E]—dc 20                                               91-20539
                                                           CIP
                                                           AC

# Ape's *Adventure*

## in Alphabet Town

You are now entering Alphabet Town,
With houses from "A" to "Z."
I'm going on an "A" adventure today,
So come along with me.

This is the "A" house of Alphabet
Town. Ape lives here.

Ape likes "a" things.

She likes to play with her

alphabet blocks.

And she likes to play her

accordion.

But most of all, she likes to make

apple pies.

One day, Ape put on her apron and
made a perfect apple pie.

When she took it out of the oven,
it looked just right. Mmmn. But it
was much too hot to eat.

"I will let my apple pie cool,"
said Ape.

And she put it on her back porch.

Then she sat in the shade of the

apple tree

and fell fast asleep.

When Ape awoke, she went to look
at her pie.

But the apple pie was gone!
Not one piece was left.

Ape was very angry.

"Who ate my apple pie?" she asked. But no one answered.

She asked her friend, the

actress,

"Do you know who ate my apple pie?"

"Not I," said the actress. "I was acting at the time."

Then Ape asked her friend, the

acrobat,

"Who ate my apple pie?"

"Not I," said the acrobat. "I was swinging in the trees at the time."

Next Ape asked her friend, the

artist,

"Who ate my apple pie?"

"Not I," said the artist. "I like only acorn pie."

Just then, Ape saw her friend, the

alligator.

She asked him, "Who ate my apple
pie?"

"Not I," said the alligator. "I was asleep. But I have always admired your apple pies."

By now it was late in the afternoon.
Ape sat on her back porch.

Just then, along came a tiny

ant.

"Did you eat my apple pie?" asked Ape.
"I am much too small to eat an apple
pie," said the ant.

"That's why I asked my friends to help." Along came the other ants from the anthill.

"Thank you for the apple pie," said
the ants. "May we have another?"

Ape began to laugh and laugh. "All right, all right," said Ape. "I will bake another apple pie." And she did.

But this time, she asked her friends
to share it with her. This time, she
knew who ate her apple pie.

# MORE FUN WITH APE

## What's in a Name?

In my "a" adventure, you read many "a" words. My name begins with an "A." Many of my friends' names begin with "A" too. Here are a few.

Anne    Angelo    Amy    Anita

Andrew    Allison    Alan    Adam

Do you know other names that start with "A"?
Does your name start with "A"?

# Ape's Word Hunt

I like to hunt for words with "a" in them. Can you help me find the words on this page that begin with "a"? How many are there?

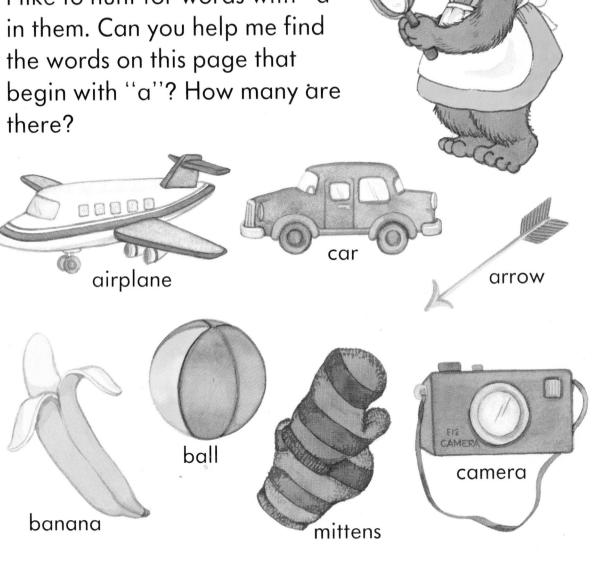

airplane

car

arrow

banana

ball

mittens

camera

Can you find any words with "a" in the middle?
Can you find any with "a" at the end?
Can you find a word with no "a"?

### Ape's Favorite Things

"A" is my favorite letter. I love "a" things. Can you guess why? You can find some of my favorite "a" things in my house on page 7. How many "a" things can you find there? Can you think of more "a" things?

Now you make up an "a" adventure.